THE RIDICULOUSLY SIMPLE GUIDE TO GOOGLE APPS (G SUITE)

A PRACTICAL GUIDE TO GOOGLE DRIVE, GOOGLE DOCS, GOOGLE SHEETS, GOOGLE SLIDES, AND GOOGLE FORMS

SCOTT LA COUNTE

RIDICULOUSLY
SIMPLE BOOKS

ANAHEIM, CALIFORNIA

www.RidiculouslySimpleBooks.com

Table of Contents

Disclaimer: *Please note, while every effort has been made to ensure accuracy, this book is not endorsed by Alphabet, Inc. and should be considered unofficial.*

INTRODUCTION

Chances are you grew up a Word and Office user. Maybe you were a rebel and committed your herd to OpenOffice, or, dare I say, WordPerfect—but for the majority of people, our lives were loyal to Microsoft.

In 2005, a small little startup named Upstartle developed something unheard of at the time: a web-based word processor called Writely. It pioneered the idea of writing on the "cloud" and changed the way people thought about word processing.

Google noticed the little upstart, and in 2006, they acquired the company. The software was abandoned and turned into what everyone knows today as Google Docs. It disrupted the industry—namely, Microsoft's industry.

Today, Google has a whole suite of productivity apps; from documents to spreadsheets, you can do just about anything from the cloud. Microsoft and Apple have each made big attempts to create cloud-based environments of their own for office productivity, but Google pioneered the idea and its collaborative, online environment make it hard to beat. It's become so feature-rich that many businesses are finding it to be the preferred way to conduct business.

If you are thinking about making the switch to Google, or have already made the switch but want to make sure you are using it correctly, then this guide will walk you through it. It will show you all the basic features to make sure you can get up and running as quick as possible.

Let's get started!

PART 1: GOOGLE DRIVE

[1]

THE GOOGLE DRIVE CRASH COURSE

This chapter will cover:
- Why is it free?
- Creating files
- Finding files

Why Is It Free?

You are probably wondering "If it's so great then why is it free?" You don't give away great software for free, right? There has to be a catch! There's always a catch! Are they taking your data and selling it on the black market? First, no!

Second, not everyone is out to get you, so just simmer down!

The Google you know gives all their tools away. How exactly do they make money? Does some rich guy donate a penny every time someone Googles "cute cat photos"? Definitely not—no one is that wealthy! Google makes money by selling ads, cloud services, selling apps, and a number of other things which all adds up to billions of dollars.

So there are ads in Google Docs? Nope! It all goes back to Google's business model. Unlike Microsoft, who is trying to make money off its software, Google is trying to make money off its service. It wants schools and businesses to use its enterprise services.

The Google Docs that we use is free; but for businesses that want to add dozens of workers, or schools who want to add hundreds of students, there is a charge.

If you are a small business, then there's a good chance you could probably make do with the free version. Plus, if Google is managing your company's email account, then you are paying for the service already.

Google Drive Overview

Every computer has "local" storage, which is where all the stuff (files, photos, documents), is stored directly on the computer. Windows computers have File/System Explorer, Mac Computers have Finder, and Google has Google Drive—it's the same concept you are accustomed to on your home computer, but it's all online.

Google Drive is basically an online version of a file directory; whatever you create in Google is stored here—think of it like Google's version of DropBox. In fact, you can also store files here—photos, videos, PDFs—whatever you want.

To get started, go to drive.google.com. If you are not signed in to a Google account, then you'll be greeted by a lovely screen that looks a little like the one below:

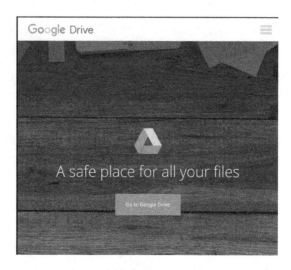

Click that "Go to Google Drive" blue button and you'll see an option that looks like the below:

While Google Docs is free to use, you do need a Google account to use it. So that's the catch, right? Free to use, but you have to pay to get a Google account? Nope! A Google account is also free. If you use Gmail, then you already have one, and can use that to sign in.

Once you are all signed in you'll see the main interface. The side pane is your main navigation. This is where you will see all of your folders. It's probably empty right now, unless you've started using it.

Two things to note here:
1. Shared with me—if people share documents or folders with you, they'll be here unless you move them.

2. Starred—to help you stay organized, you can "star" documents. When you "star" them, they will still be in your main directory, but they'll be here as well.

If you have the basic free plan, you'll have 15 GBs of storage. That's obviously a lot. Considering that a document is very small, you'll probably never want more—unless you are also using Google Drive to store videos and files, or to back up your entire computer.

Why on Earth would you want to pay to back up your computer on the cloud? Because it's surprising cheap! The rates below are what you can expect—they might go up after this book is printed, but not by much since they've been this low for a while.

Most people have around 200 GBs of data float-ing around. That means, for less than a dinner for two at Olive Garden, you can safely know that your data is protected online!

Why back it up online? Two reasons:

1. What if your house floods or burns down and you don't have time to get your com-puter. Think of all the memories you would lose that are stored on your com-puter.

2. What if you are away on business or a family trip and you really need a docu-ment. It's safely online and you can ac-cess it anytime.

If you want to back up your entire computer to Google Drive, you just need to download some software that will sync your computer to the cloud. That means if you save a new file, that file automat-ically goes to the cloud and you don't have to do a thing. You can also pick and choose what folders are synced to the cloud. To get the software, go to the address below:

https://support.google.com/drive/an-swer/2424368?co=GENIE.Platform%3DDesk-tDD&hl=en

Creating Files and Docs

Once you're ready to create either a document (such as a doc, spreadsheet or presentation), click the new button in the left menu pane:

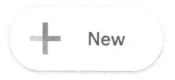

This will bring up several choices. The main three apps are on the bottom of this menu, but if you click "more" you can see some of the useful, but lesser used, Google Apps (I'm looking at you Google Jamboard!). You can also access this menu by right- clicking inside Google Drive:

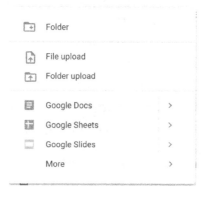

This is also where you'll go to upload files from your computer, or to create a new folder.

Creating folders will help you stay organized. You may, for example, have a recipe folder, or school folder, or a bills folder—you can have as many folders as you want. You can also create folders inside folders (and folders inside the folder you just created inside the folder—go ahead and figure that sentence out...I'll wait!). It's just like file organization on your computer.

If you want to create a folder within a folder, you can either open that folder up and select the new button, or you can right-click inside that open folder and select "Folder."

Starring and Sharing Files

Once the docs are created, you'll be able to right-click them at any time to bring up a new menu that's just for that specific file. You can add a star to it, rename it, preview it, and, of course, share it.

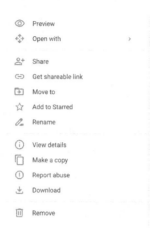

Once you click "Get sharable link" (the option for sharing a file with other people), you'll see something a little like this:

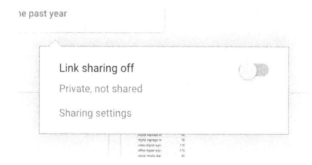

If it's white, like the above, it will note that sharing is off. To turn it on, just click that white box, and it will turn green and note that sharing is turned on. It will also give you a link to the document.

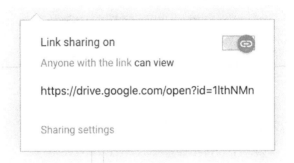

When it's on, by default, it's a non-public link. That means the only way someone is going to find it is if you give them the link.

If you click "Sharing settings" you'll get a few more options. You can email a person the link and also make them an editor, or give them all access.

Click the "Anyone with the link can view" drop down and you can manage the access, for example, if you only want certain people that you email to see it—note: if you select this option, they will need to be signed into a Google Account (the one you used in the email name in the box under this), to see the doc.

If you select "More" you'll have a few more options. One is to make the file public. This means it's going to be searchable to anyone on Google and people may find it randomly—people you don't know—so it's best if you don't make your Google Sheet with the names and phone numbers of "People with excessive gas" public.

Find Files

Files are pretty easy to find when you are first getting started. But they add up quickly—especially if you are using them for school or business, or if you are backing up all the files on your computer.

Fortunately, Google has a search bar that works remarkably well—it's right on top of Google Drive. You don't have to know the name of the file—you can search for what's in the document. So if you can't remember what you named your Google Doc, but you know it had the line "And that is why I love competitive dog grooming" (yes, it's a thing!), then just type in that phrase and it will find your doc.

If it's returning too many results—because you have obviously written countless scholarly papers on the subject of competitive dog grooming—then click that little arrow next to the search bar.

That brings up an advanced search. You'll be able to search by owner, by those that are starred, when it was lasted opened, what kind of file it is, and more. Once you've added in all your filters, just hit search, and it will return results in seconds.

PART 2: GOOGLE DOCS

[1]

GOOGLE DOCS CRASH COURSE

This chapter will cover:
- Why use Word?
- The Crash Course
- Getting Started

Should I Throw Away Word and Never Look Back?

Before getting started, let's talk about the elephant in the room: Microsoft Word!

Does Google Docs make Word irrelevant? It really depends on the user. For most people, Google Docs can probably accomplish what you want to do.

Microsoft is paid software, but it's also a lot more powerful. If you are running macros, or doing mail mergers, and need other advanced features, then you'll probably want to stick with Word. There are add-ons for Google Docs, but they just don't beat what you'll find in the full version of Microsoft Word.

If you are just doing basic writing, then Google Docs will be just fine. When it comes to collaboration, it's more than just fine; while Microsoft has made great strides towards making it easier to share and collaborate in Word, Google is the one who mastered the idea. Google also has plug-ins for editing tools such as Grammarly, and is making a big push to be more responsive to catching basic grammatical errors.

Personally, I use Google Docs almost daily, but I still have a copy of Word on my desktop, and that's what I use for my final draft. Once collaboration is finished, I copy and paste it into Word and apply all the final touches.

The Crash Course

Before we jump into creating our first document, I'll go over the main Google Docs toolbar. If you've ever used Word, then you'll probably know what most of these do already. If you ever get stuck, then hover over the icon and it will give you a description of what it does.

The first two icons are your undo, redo icons. This undoes or redoes whatever you just typed:

Next is the Print, spellcheck, and formatter. You probably know what the first two are. The last one is a handy little tool; it copies the format of the text. So let's say I have text that is bold, 14- point in size. I can highlight that text, select the paint roller, then click on the text I want to apply the style to. Instantly that text is changed to the same style.

The 100% is the zoom. If you want to zoom out to see more (but smaller) text on the screen, then click on that:

100% ▼

Fonts and style is next to that. This is where you can select the style (if it's a Heading, for example), the font family, the font size, and if you want to bold, italicize, underline, or change the color of the text.

The insert options is the next section. These are all the things you may want to insert into a doc. That includes a link, a comment, and an image:

Justification is next to that. If you want to right align, center align, or change the line spacing, you'll use these options:

If you want to create a numbered or bulleted list, you can use the next two icons; next to those are the indentation:

If you have formatting you want to reset, you can use the icon below. This is good if you've copied text from the web and you want to reset it to the default Google Docs text size:

The last two options change how you are viewing a document and to hide the toolbar:

That's a high-level overview. These things will make more sense as we go.

Getting Started

Okay, so how exactly do you use Google Docs? There are several ways, but the quickest is to just type in drive.google.com.

Once you have your Google account, then you are all set. Repeat the step above and the browser Window should look more like the below:

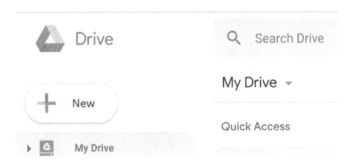

Docs really shines through its connection to Google Drive. Anything you start in Google Docs is automatically saved in your Google Drive account—no need to worry about losing work through power failures, device catastrophes, or really just about any other scenario. Changes are saved as you go, and so are the various versions of your document, so it's easy to revert to an earlier stage of a draft if you need to.

[3]

YOUR FIRST DOCUMENT

This chapter will cover:
- Creating your first document
- Titling your Google Doc
- Opening saved docs

Creating Your First Doc

Now that you have your account, let's create a document. Click on the "New" button and then hover over Google Docs; there are two options: Black document and From a template. For now, select "From a template." I'll cover templates a little bit later.

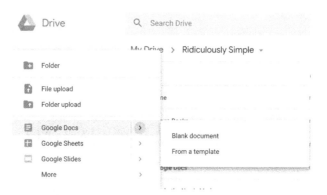

This is going to open up a new tab, and your Google Docs editor will appear.

If you're a Word or Pages user, then you'll be relieved to know everything is designed to work the same way. Many of the buttons look identical.

So, you don't need this book, right?! There's still a difference, and that's what we'll spend the most time with in this book.

Let's have some fun. Pretend the American Revolution is taking place in the year 2019 instead of the year 1776. The British have put fines on our beloved Internet usage, and the people have had enough! Why should you have to pay to see videos of adorable puppies on skateboards?

Michelle Obama is the leader of the American colonies. She's been working on the first draft of a proclamation with her first man, Barack Obama.

The first thing she needs is a title.

How to title your Google Doc

Look up in the upper left-hand corner of your Google Docs editor. See the text field that says, "Untitled Document." That's every Google Docs default title. Click on it.

You can now add any title you want by typing. I'll pick something highly original: "The Declaration of Independence," but you can pick anything you want. When you finish, hit the enter key.

In a flash, watch that top bar change with your new title. As long as it shows the new title, then it worked.

Need even more assurance? Look to the right of it: it should say "All changes saved"? Guess what?! It saved!

All changes saved in Drive

It may not seem all that revolutionary today, but everything saves automatically. You don't need to hit CTRL S every few seconds. Google saves as you type. If you are the paranoid type, then you still can save manually.

Let's start things off by creating a headline for our doc. Let's go crazy and use Corsiva, 18-point font. You only live once, right?

This hopefully feels familiar to you—it's essentially the same way you do it in other document editors. I bet you've used this type of toolbar hundreds of times before. Here's the take away here: icons that look like they do in another app tend to do the exact same thing they did in that other app.

My Glorious Heading!

So let's write the title and first paragraph of our declaration, then in a moment we'll send it off for review.

Everything is looking good so far, right? But what happens if there's a power outage? In a blink of a second, it all goes dark. How do we get back to where we left off?

Opening a saved document
Close your browser. Make sure Google Docs has completely gone away.

Now go right back to drive.google.com.

Unless you are on a public computer (like at a library), Google will show you all the files you have created. Since it was the last thing you worked on, you should see The Declaration of Independence right at the top in the Quick Access list.

If you are just getting started, it will also be the only doc you see, and you can access it below the quick access; it will look a "little" like this:

I say "little" because you might be in list view or you might be in grid view. What's the difference? List view looks like the above—it gives the name, who the owner is, and the time it was edited. Grid view is more of a thumbnail preview of the doc, like this:

The Declaration of Independ...

Notice how author and time lasted edited is gone?

What's better? It's a preference, but if you are working with dozens of documents, then Grid view probably will not be ideal unless you need to see previews.

To toggle between the two, click these icons in the upper corner:

List is the horizontal lines, and grid is the six square boxes.

The top spot goes to documents that have been recently edited.

When you double-click on "The Declaration of Independence," it opens up in a new tab. It's basically the same as opening a document back up in Word—the difference: It's in the cloud.

You can also right-click it to see more options—one of them is "Open with" and you can open it by clicking Google Docs.

This option would be useful if you have a Chromebook that has other editing tools installed and you don't want to use Google Docs to edit it. For it to work, however, you need to have those other apps installed.

You can do that by going to the Chrome extensions store:

https://chrome.google.com/webstore/category/extensions

This is a marketplace for all things Chrome, and most of the extensions (or apps) are free. Just make sure you are using Chrome—hence the name. If you aren't, you can still see the page, but you'll be greeted with this subtle notice:

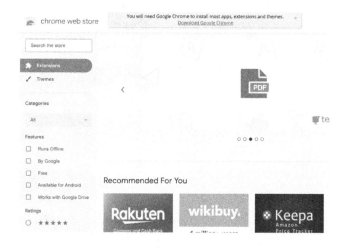

Like most Word Processing editors today, if you open it on a different device (i.e. smartphone or tablet), it's going to look pretty similar. Anything you change on those devices will reflect the document everywhere. It's all in the cloud.

Users of mobile devices (such as iPhones and iPads) can see Google Docs will need a native app to make edits, but what I'm talking about in this book is essentially identical on the apps.

Unfortunately, you'll need a separate app for every app you are using. So you need to get the Google Drive app and the Google Docs app—and if you plan on using Google Slides or Sheets, you'll need to get those apps too. Fortunately, they're free.

Your device has an app store, and that's where you'll download them—just type in the name of the app. The exception here is Fire tablets; these tablets have a not-so-nice relationship with Google that I won't go into here. Google won't put their apps in the app store because of that not-so-nice relationship. You can still install them, but you would need to do something called "side load app." That basically means you are downloading the app onto an SD card, putting the card into the tablet, and installing it manually. I'm not covering how to do that in this book, but if installing it on a Fire device is a must, then there are plenty of tutorials for that. Do so at your own risk, as it's not exactly supported by the device.

[4]

SHARING IS CARING

This chapter will cover:
- How to share docs
- Editing and collaborating

How To Share Your Google Docs

Google Docs is hands-down one of the easiest ways to work on a group document.

When two or more people are editing a document at the same time, you'll be able to see that person's cursor position and watch edits in real time. If you're concerned about losing work, remember that Google Docs saves the version history for you, so it's easy to revert if you need to. Click File > See revision history (or press CTRL+ALT+SHIFT+G). By default, revisions are shown grouped into daily periods, but if you want to see changes made by the minute, click "Show more detailed revisions" at the bottom of the revisions panel. You can see which collaborator made each change in a group document. Of course, the slightly less elegant Undo and Redo functions are always available as well!

Back to your masterpiece in progress: The Declaration of Independence. Michelle is ready for a second opinion of what she's done.

She knows Barack is a master orator, so she knows he's going to have some good input.

Look up in the upper right corner. See the blue button that says Share? Click on that. It's going to open up several different sharing options.

There's a few ways to share it:
1. Type their email address and let Google do the rest.
2. Manually (covered below).

Share with others   Get shareable link ⊖

People

Enter names or email addresses...

Done   Advanced

When you email someone, you can also manage exactly what they can do. Click that little pencil icon. By default, it will say they can edit the doc. You can change it so they can only comment on the doc, or they can only view the doc:

✓ Can edit
Can comment
Can view

You can also hit advance at the bottom of the share menu, and have a few more features—such as disabling print:

But let's say you don't want to email the first man. Let's say you just want to give him a link—that way he doesn't need to use his Google account to open it. To do that, follow the steps above, but in the upper corner of the box, click "Get shareable link."

Get shareable link 🔗

Once you click that, it will give you a sharable link—it even copies the link so if you hit CTRL-V (or right-click paste) you can paste that link anywhere you want.

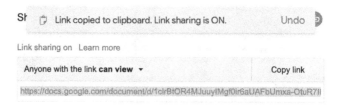

If you click on can view, it will give you a drop-down menu with more features. It looks sort of like the other drop-down menu above, but there's an option that says "more."

When you click on "More," it gives you a few extra features—such as making the document public in search engines so anyone can find it.

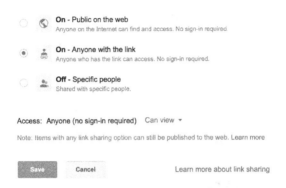

You can turn sharing off at any time, by hitting the "Share" button; once it's turned off, anyone who goes to that link—even if they've been there before—won't be able to see it. If you've emailed a person, they are still a viewer until you remove them.

If you have a person who really hates Google Docs and refuses to view your document in anything but Word, Google Docs allows you to export your work to a Word Document so you don't have to do all of the copying and font processing yourself. Just click on file > download as > Word; there's a whole host of other exports here as well.

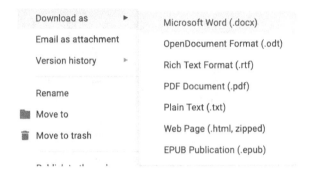

Editing and Collaborating with Others

Let's pretend for a moment the first man is in the document and he's ready to make some changes and add some notes.

As he goes through the document, he's going to make some notes. There are a few ways to do it; the easiest way is to right-click and select "Comment."

You can also get this, by selecting Insert on the toolbar, and Comment:

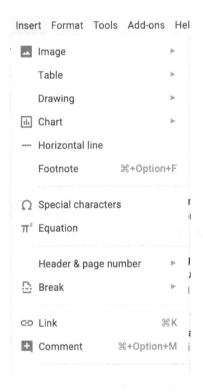

Either of these will bring up the comment box. Add your comment, and select the blue comment box when you are ready to post it. When you add a comment (or make a change), it's in real-time; that means if the person who is collaborating with you has the document open, they can actually watch you make the edits and add the comments.

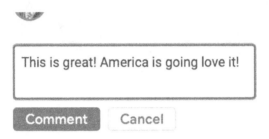

If you have multiple people working on the doc, you can type "@" and see a list of people you can mention; if you mention them, Google will notify them so they can add a reply to your comment.

Once the comment is posted, it will show up on the side of Google Docs.

ph

our

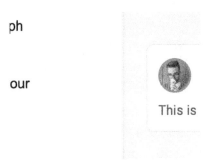

This is

You can delete or edit the comment by clicking on those three little dots on the side of the box:

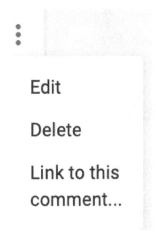

Edit

Delete

Link to this comment...

The person on the other end will be able to re-solve the comment (that makes it disappear, but they can undo it).

Or they can reply to it.

When others are editing a doc I created, my personal preference is to tell them to edit with suggestions. This lets me see the changes they have made. You can turn it on by clicking on the pencil icon in the menu, and selecting "Suggesting."

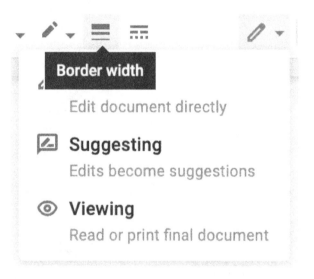

Now when they edit the doc, it will show up as a different color.

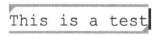

If you click on what they changed, you can accept the change with the check mark, or ignore it with the X. You can also ask questions about it and they can reply.

To see all the versions of a document, go to "file" and see versions.

If there is going to be a lot of versions, then one suggestion is to name each one—which you can do here.

When you click "See version history", you'll get a list of all the versions. Clicking on any one of them will bring up that version. You can view it, or even restore it.

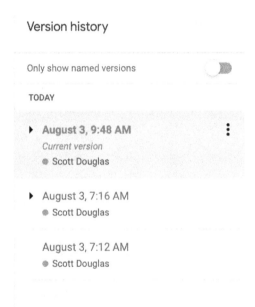

To get back to the document, just hit the back button in the menu (not the browser back button):

[5]

BEYOND THE BASICS

This chapter will cover:
- Printing
- Adding photos
- Adding tables
- Adding spreadsheets
- Adding a table of contents
- Templates

Printing From the Cloud

Michelle's pretty happy with her declaration, but she's still a little old school—she likes to read through her work the old fashion way with that little thing called paper. So, she obviously needs to print it.

You probably can guess that you do this a way you are familiar with: File > Print.

From here, it gets a little...complicated. Printing is not something Google Docs excels at.

You have two main options:

Save it to your computer and then print it from your computer.

Add your computer to Google

If you want to add your computer to Google Cloud print, then click the link.

It will walk you through the steps. The steps change depending on the kind of printer you have. It's not rocket science, but you'll need to pay attention to details.

If you want to skip the fuss there's a longer, but less hassle, way: export as a PDF, open the PDF on your computer, print it from your computer. Because you already have a printer on your computer, it will show up when you do File > Print.

Adding Photos to Google Docs

Okay, so you've printed it, you've agreed the text is where you want it to be by collaborating with others—now you want to jazz it up.

Google Docs works just like any other word processor. You can add in images wherever you want, either by copying and pasting, or by adding them in from Insert > Image.

Just find a place where you want to add an image. If you have found the image online and copied it, then just do CTRL-V, and it will be added in.

If you have the image stored on your computer, in your Google Drive, or any number of other places, then you can do one of two things. One: click Insert > Image:

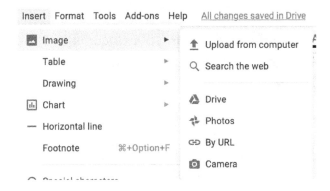

Or, two, click the Picture icon in the toolbar:

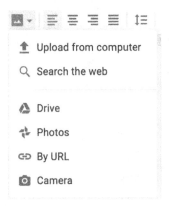

If you simply want to add the image from your computer, then choose "Upload from computer" and find it on your computer. You can also search the web for the file, paste a link to the file, or, if you are using a device that supports it, use the computer's built-in camera to add an image.

Once the image is in your document, click on it. You'll see little blue squares around it—and a small blue dot:

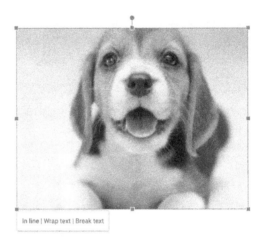

In line | Wrap text | Break text

Clicking on these lets you resize the image; clicking on the dot will let you rotate the image. You can also choose how the text communicates with the image. By default, it will be Inline—that means the text will go above and below it. "Wrap text" will mean the text will go on all sides of it. "Break text" lets you put a margin around the text—if you want a little white space, for example.

If you right-click, you'll also see some extra options for the image:

Most options you probably understand. "Alt text" is handy if you'll be publishing this online—it is text that shows if the text can't be seen; you are basically describing the image.

Clicking on "Image options" will bring up even more options:

🖼 Image Options ✕

Recolor

No Recolor ▾

Adjustments

Transparency

Brightness

Contrast

Reset

Here you can make it brighter, for example; you can also make it semi-transparent—which is great if you will be using it as a watermark.

If you change your mind about the image, you can delete it or you can just click "Replace image" when you click on it:

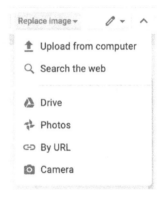

Getting Really Fancy

We have photos. It's looking snazzy, right?! Now let's dig in deeper.

Next, we are going to learn how to add in tables and spreadsheets. This might not be for everyone, but it's still good to know.

First, let's see how to do this the manual way. This is a good option if you don't have a lot of data you are working with—let's pretend here that you want to show the week's lunch menu.

Go to "Insert" on the toolbar and "Table":

From here, you'll drag the number of boxes based on how big you want your table to be. This is a lunch menu, and I'm going to make it seven days with two rows.

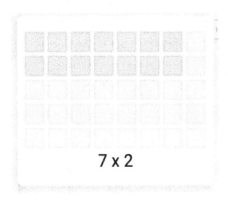

7 x 2

It will show up blank:

Next, I'll add in my menu. I'm personally excited for Saturday, where lunch will be a bag of Doritos—I really put a lot of effort into that lunch!

Sunday	Monday	Tuesday	Wednesday	Thursday	Friday	Saturday
Green eggs and ham	Lobster	Hamburger	Lambchops	Fish & Chips	FREE DAY	Bag of doritos

That table is nice, but it doesn't really visually illustrate anything. Next, I'm going to change the color of the top row so it stands out a bit more. Highlight that entire top row:

Sunday	Monday	Tuesday	Wednesday	Thursday	Friday	Saturday
Green	Lobster	Hamburger	Lambchops	Fish &	FREE DAY	Bag of

Next, right-click, which will bring up your "Table" menu. Select "Table properties." This kind of sounds like the properties for the entire table, but because we highlighted and then right-clicked, it will only change the style of the row highlighted (if we had right-clicked without highlighting, it would have changed everything).

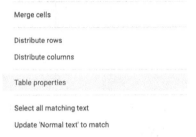

There's a lot of properties here, but the one we want for this row is "Cell background color":

Once you change the background, click "OK" and the table will look similar to the below:

Sunday	Monday	Tuesday	Wednesday	Thursday	Friday	Saturday
Green eggs and ham	Lobster	Hamburger	Lambchops	Fish & Chips	FREE DAY	Bag of doritos

You can also highlight one row and change the color. I'll change Friday because it's a free day and I want it to stand out more.

Let's pretend we don't want cow meat this week—we want two days of lobster! Delete "hamburger," highlight both the Monday and Tuesday boxes, right-click, and select "merge cells":

Merge cells

Distribute rows

The cell is now one box:

Sunday	Monday	Tuesday	Wednesday	Thursday	Friday	Saturday
Green eggs and ham	Lobster		Lambchops	Fish & Chips	FREE DAY	Bag of doritos

Now, let's make that menu a little taller. Right-click, "select table properties," and check off

"Minimum row height." I'll make it one inch. This means if the text is longer, it could be more than 1 inch, but it will be at least one inch:

Dimensions (inches)

☐ Column width

☑ Minimum row height   1

Cell padding   0.069

Table alignment

Center ▾

Left indent (inches)   0

Sunday	Monday	Tuesday	Wednesday	Thursday	Friday	Saturday
Green eggs and ham	Lobster	Lambchops		Fish & Chips	FREE DAY	Bag of doritos

We almost have the menu where we want it, but there's still a little work to be done. Let's make the cells show the text in the middle of the cell. Go to "Table properties" and under "Cell Vertical Alignment," select "middle":

Cell vertical alignment

Top

Middle

Bottom

Now everything is evenly aligned in the middle:

Sunday	Monday	Tuesday	Wednesday	Thursday	Friday	Saturday
Green eggs and ham	Lobster		Lambchops	Fish & Chips	FREE DAY	Bag of doritos

Right now, all the columns are the same width. You can make the table larger by dragging either end of the table:

Sunday	Monday	Tuesday	Wednesday	Thursday	Friday	Saturday
Green eggs and ham	Lobster		Lambchops	Fish & Chips	FREE DAY	Bag of doritos

How to insert spreadsheets from Google Sheet

Google Docs integrates all things Google into it. Let's take that to heart and look at another Google app quickly: Google Sheets.

Go ahead and go back to drive.google.com and create a new document—this time a spreadsheet (hint: click the new button and then select spreadsheet)

In a flash you have a spreadsheet in the cloud. All the menus are pretty similar to Google Docs, and you enter text the same way.

For this example, I'm going to use a library database that's already been created. Let's pretend I want to copy some of it (though I could also do all of it) into my Google Doc. I just need to highlight what I want to copy, then either right-click and choose "copy" or do CTRL-C on the keyboard.

Next, I'll go back into my Google Doc and hit CTRL-V on the keyboard to paste it. It's going to ask us if we want to paste it in Linked or unlinked:

Paste table

⦿ Link to spreadsheet
Only editors can update the table. Collaborators can see a link to the source spreadsheet.

◯ Paste unlinked

Learn more   Cancel   Paste

What's the difference? Linked lets a person go to that original spreadsheet—they can view other rows and make changes. Unlinked pastes it in as a new table and if you make changes to the spreadsheet, it won't show up in your Google Doc.

I'm going to pick Linked. It will paste in and look pretty...basic:

A brief history of time	Stephen W. Hawking	Hawking, Stephen W.	Bantam Books		Astronomy	198	QB981 .H377 1988
A Career as an Electrician	Daniel E. Harmon	Harmon, Daniel E.	The Rosen Publishing Group, Inc	2010	Juvenile Nonfiction	80	TK159 .H37 2011
A Child's Garden of Verses	Robert Louis Stevenson	Stevenson, Robert Louis	Chronicle Books	1989	Juvenile Nonfiction	30	PR548 9 .C5 1989
A Concise Guide to Technical Communication	Laura J. Gurak, John M. Lannon	Gurak, Laura J.	Pearson/Long man	2004	Technology & Engine ering	17	T10.5 .G83 2004
A Concise Public Speaking Handbook	Steven A. Beebe, Susan J. Beebe	Beebe, Steven A.	Allyn & Bacon		Perfor ming Arts	292	PN412 9.15 .B42 2012
					Techno		TK786

Just like the table we created earlier, however, you can go in and create all sorts of styles for it. For example, I chose "table property" and changed the background color for the first two rows:

These changes don't show up in the original spreadsheet.

So let's pretend that you also linked your sheet into Google Docs. If you click on the link button in the upper corner, then you'll get new options:

You can unlink the document, for example, or open it. If sharing is not turned on, the other person won't be able to access it.

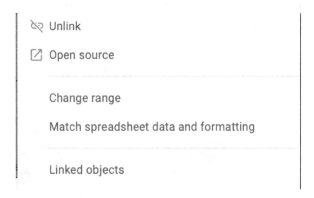

There's a Template for that

Once you know your way around Google Docs, you can save time by using one of the pre-created Google Templates for Docs. To use one, go to drive.google.com and create a Google Doc—but instead of blank, select from template.

A new window is going to open with all of your options. Unlike Word and Pages, Google isn't huge on templates, but they do allow others to add templates, and you can find plenty of others by doing a quick Google search for Google Docs templates.

Table of Contents

One useful feature is the table of contents. This would more commonly be used in a book or long-form document. You hopefully won't use it to share a love letter with your wife, but you might want to use it if you are using Google Docs for a dissertation.

You can see/add the table of contents by going to Insert > Table of contents. You can do it either with or without the page numbers:

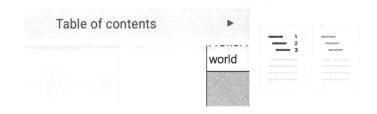

If you don't see your table of contents after adding it, there's likely a good reason: you haven't added any headings to the Doc.

Click on Normal text from your drop down. See all the different options?

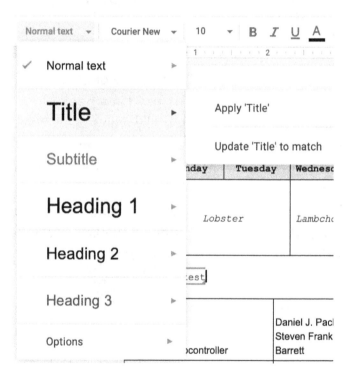

If this were a book, then "Title" would be the title on the first page. "Heading 1" would be the chapter title, "Heading 2" and "Heading 3" would be sections within that chapter.

For each one you can select "Update 'Title' to match." Let's say "Title" changes the text to size 24 but you want it to be size 36. If you change your text to size 36, then highlight it and select "Title" and update it. Then, every time you add a new Title in the doc (not other docs) it will update it to that style.

If you want it to apply to every doc going forward, then go to "Options" in that same section and select "Save as my default styles":

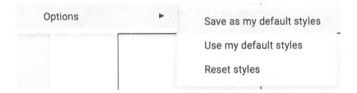

[5]

THIS AND THAT

This chapter will cover:
- Google Docs menus

In this section, I'll cover some final things you need to know about Google Docs. This isn't comprehensive—I'm not going to cover Script Editor, for example, because the point is to keep things simple and show you the features you'll most likely be using.

File menu

We've covered all the important things in the file menu, but there's one thing of note: File > Language:

By default, it will be in English; that means if you start typing a document in Spanish, then you'll see all kinds of grammatical errors. Changing the language adds in a new dictionary so it doesn't think you are just typing gibberish.

View Menu

There are two things I'll point out under the View menu. First, Print layout. By default, it's checked off. Clicking it will show the document in a long scroll view—so no page breaks:

"Show document online" will bring up a side panel to show all the headers in your document:

Insert Menu

If you want to add a header (such as every page has your last name on top), or add in page number, then head to "Insert" and "Header & page number."

Insert > Break will add in a page break. By default, Google does this automatically, but if you are doing a new section that you want on a new page, then you can do it manually here:

Insert > Special characters is where you can grab symbols like the © sign:

Ω Special characters

Insert > Bookmark is helpful in longer documents. You can create bookmark links, so whenever you are referencing something, you can send them right to that section so they don't have to scroll to find it:

Bookmark

Tools Menu
The tools menu is where you'll find Spell checker and word count.

Tools   Add-ons   Help   All changes saved in Drive

Spelling and grammar   ▶

Word count   ⌘+Shift+C

You can also see the built in dictionary and where you can translate the document into another language. I should note here that this is obviously a computer translation, so don't expect perfection.

Dictionary   ⌘+Shift+Y

Translate document

🎤 Voice typing   ⌘+Shift+S

"Explore" is helpful in research papers. It keeps you in the doc so you don't have to go to a tab to look something up:

⭐ Explore   ⌘+Option+Shift+I

In the below example, I typed in "Stephen Colbert" and it gave me basic information about him in a side menu:

Add-ons Menu

This is where you can add on extensions if you don't go to the Google store:

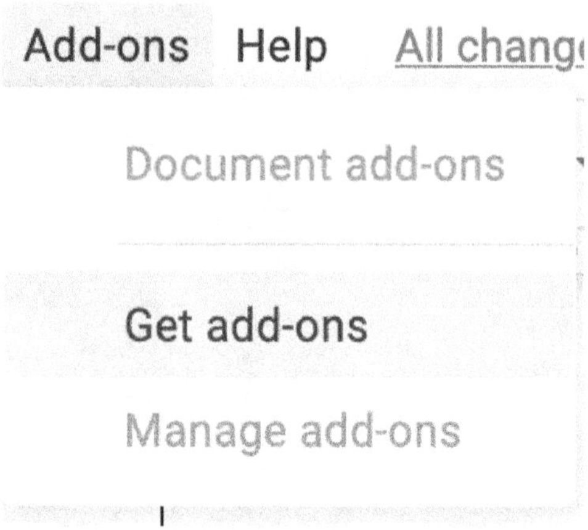

Add-ons   Help   All change

Document add-ons

Get add-ons

Manage add-ons

Help Menu

And finally, the help menu will let you search for common tasks, see updates to Google Docs, and even get training:

Help   All changes saved in Drive

Search the menus (Option+/)

Docs Help

Training

Updates

Report a problem

Report abuse/copyright

⌨ Keyboard shortcuts   ⌘/

[6]

GOOGLE DOCS KEYBOARD SHORTCUTS

You can see all the keyboard shortcuts in Google Docs by selecting Help > Keyboard shortcuts.

For your reference, below are some of the most common ones you'll use.

Common actions

Copy	Ctrl + c
Cut	Ctrl + x
Paste	Ctrl + v
Paste without formatting	Ctrl + Shift + v
Undo	Ctrl + z
Redo	Ctrl + Shift + z
Insert or edit link	Ctrl + k
Print	Ctrl + p

Open	Ctrl + o
Find	Ctrl + f
Find and replace	Ctrl + h
Text formatting	
Bold	Ctrl + b
Italicize	Ctrl + i
Underline	Ctrl + u
Strikethrough	Alt + Shift + 5
Superscript	Ctrl + .
Subscript	Ctrl + ,
Copy text formatting	Ctrl + Alt + c
Paste text formatting	Ctrl + Alt + v
Clear text formatting	Ctrl + \
Increase font size	Ctrl + Shift + >
Decrease font size	Ctrl + Shift + <
Paragraph formatting	
Increase paragraph indentation	Ctrl +]
Decrease paragraph indentation	Ctrl + [
Apply normal text style	Ctrl + Alt + 0
Apply heading style [1-6]	Ctrl + Alt + [1-6]
Left align	Ctrl + Shift + l
Center align	Ctrl + Shift + e
Right align	Ctrl + Shift + r
Justify	Ctrl + Shift + j
Numbered list	Ctrl + Shift + 7
Bulleted list	Ctrl + Shift + 8
Comments	
Insert comment	Ctrl + Alt + m
Open discussion thread	Ctrl + Alt + Shift + a
Menus	
File menu	Alt + f
Edit menu	Alt + e

88 | *The Ridiculously Simple Guide to Google Apps (G Suite)*

View menu	Alt + v
Insert menu	Alt + i
Format menu	Alt + o
Tools menu	Alt + t
Help menu	Alt + h

PART 3: GOOGLE SHEETS

[1]

GOOGLE SHEETS CRASH COURSE

This chapter will cover:
- What is Sheets?
- Should you still use Excel?
- The Google Sheets crash course

What is Google Sheets, Anyway?

For 30-some-odd years, the world of spreadsheets has been ruled by one king: Microsoft Excel. Sure, there were far away challengers that tried to overtake the beast—I'm looking at you, Lotus 1-2-3—but none have come close to dethroning the powerful tool...until Google Sheets.

So what is Google Sheets? It's a cloud-based spreadsheet. Think Excel, but online. "But Excel is online," you say. Yes! But Google was there first, and really has the advantage over Excel in this arena. It's quicker and easier to use for collaboration.

Google Sheets is also free; Excel has monthly/yearly subscriptions.

Excel vs. Google Sheets: What's Right For Me?

If you are judging Google Sheets by mere looks, you might think it was a clone. It has tabs, it has cells, and, heck, even the formulas are largely the same!

So what is the difference?!

Let's go with the obvious one. As of this writing, you can add 5,000,000 cells to Google Sheets; Microsoft Excel? 17,179,869,184 cells.

How embarrassing, right? How on Earth can you get anything done with only 5,000,000 cells!

Kidding aside, that number does tell you one thing: Excel is the best software for large corporations managing budgets spanning dozens of years. But for the rest of us, that number really doesn't matter. A spreadsheet with 5,000,000 cells is plenty. The moment you get to cell 5,000,001 you have hopefully made it in the world and have sold your business. You now live on a private island where you ride llamas bareback on the beach. Why llamas? Because you are ridiculously wealthy and horses just seem too middleclass.

There is one other thing that's telling about that number, however. It's speed.

What do I mean by that? The reason Google limits cells is because in a cloud-based environment, the more cells you add, the slower it gets. Excel can afford crazy amounts of cells because it's locally installed. As long as you have a good computer with plenty of memory, you can have a nearly endless number of cells and not have to worry about things slowing down.

Again, most of us probably don't care about speed. We're working with smaller spreadsheets and never notice lags. But, and it's a big but, things do slow down when you start working with thousands of cells in Google, and that can be problematic for productivity.

The biggest reason people are switching to Google Sheets, however, is collaboration. Google is king when it comes to collaboration. If you are working on a budget with a group of people, then Google is hands down the way to go.

The Google Sheets Crash Course

The first three buttons are pretty straightforward: undo, redo what you have typed and print. The last one is the format painter; this lets you copy the style of one cell into another cell. To use it, click the cell you want to copy, select the format painter, and then click the cell you want to put the style in.

By default, a spreadsheet is viewed at 100%; if you are working with a larger sheet and want to see more cells on your screen, you can use this to zoom out—or also to zoom in and see less cells on your screen.

The next five options tell the cell what the content is. $ turns it into currency; % turns it into a percentage; the next two move the decimals forward and backward; and finally, the 123 gives you additional options to telling the cell what it is—plain text, a scientific formula, a date, etc. This is also useful if you have a number, but you want Google to treat it like plain text.

$ % .0 .00 123 ▾

If you have used any kind of productivity software, then you should know the next two options; if you've been under a rock: this is the font and font size.

Arial ▾ | 10 ▾

Next to the font is the font formatter; here you can bold, italicize, strikethrough (i.e. put a line through the middle of the text), or change the number.

B *I* S̶ A̲

The next set of options is for the cell style; you can change the fill color, the cell border, and merge cells. To merge cells, highlight the cells you want to merge and then click this option.

Justification and placement are managed in the next four options. Here you can center/right/left align, move the content to the bottom/middle/top of the cell, wrap the text (by default text will just spill over into the next cell unless you resize the cell; this option tells it to make the text go to the next line, sort of like hitting the enter key, since the enter/return key doesn't work in Sheets); and finally rotate text, which also lets you change the direction of the text.

The last set of options is to insert things into a cell. You can insert a link, comment, chart, filter, or function.

On the far side, is an up arrow. This just hides or unhides the toolbar.

ᐱ

[2]

GETTING STARTED WITH GOOGLE SHEETS

This chapter will cover:
- Your first Sheet
- Opening saved documents
- The basics

Okay, so how exactly do you use Google Sheets? Like everything else in the Google Suite family! The beauty of Google is once you learn one, learning others is pretty easy.

Here's a refresher: type in drive.google.com.
Once you have your Google account (hopefully you do by now), then you are all set. Repeat the step above and the browser Window should look more like the below.

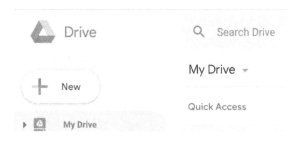

Creating Your First Sheet

Now that you have your account, let's create a document. Click on the "New" button and then hover over Google Sheets; there are two options: "Blank document" and "From a template." For now, select "From a template." I'll cover templates a little bit later.

At this point, you'll be taken to Google's Sheets editor. This is where you do the actual work. Everything is designed to function just like Excel or Numbers.

Have a look in the upper left-hand corner of your Google Sheets. You'll see a text field that says "Untitled Document." Click on that.

You will now be prompted with a box asking you to rename the document. I chose "My Glorious Google Sheet!," but you can type anything you want. When you finish, hit the enter key.

Once you do that, the top bar will change, reflecting the new name you've chosen:

My Glorious Google Sheet! | in ▓▓ My Drive
File   Edit   View   Insert   Format   Data   Tools   Add-ons   Help   All changes saved in Drive

Do you see the text on the right where it says, "All changes saved"? That's another awesome thing about Google Sheets:

All changes saved in Drive

In a stroke of pure brilliance, the folks at Google have decided to completely automate document saves. As you write, Google saves your project and tells you when it last did this. If you want, you can go ahead and save, but it's practically unnecessary. Google Sheets saves after you enter every new word.

Opening A Saved Document

Don't worry about accidently closing your tab. When you open it back up, Google will take you right back to your list of documents. You should see your document at the top of that list in "Quick Access."

If you are just getting started, it will also be the only sheet you see, and you can access it below the quick access

List view looks like the above—it gives the name, who the owner is, and the time it was edited. Grid view is more of a thumbnail preview of the Sheet.

Notice how "author" and "time lasted edited" is gone?

What's better? It's a preference, but if you are working with dozens of files, then Grid view probably will not be ideal unless you need to see previews.

To toggle between the two, click these icons in the upper corner:

List is the horizontal lines, and grid is the six square boxes.

The most recently viewed and edited files gets the top spot.

When you double-click on the Sheet or document you want, it'll open right up in the browser, and we can get back to writing. It's just like opening up an Excel or Numbers document on your home computer.

The Basics

Now that we've gotten our quick crash course, let's add some numbers and see how this thing works.

I'll start by adding some years; like any good spreadsheet software, Google is pretty good at guessing. If there's a pattern, then you can autofill the cells. In the example below, I've added two years: 1900 and 1901. When I highlight those two cells, there's a tiny blue box:

	A
1	Year
2	1900
3	1901

If I drag that blue box down, Google will correctly predict that I am putting years in and add one year per cell for as long as I drag:

	A
1	Year
2	1900
3	1901
4	1902
5	1903
6	1904
7	1905
8	1906
9	1907
10	1908
11	1909
12	1910
13	

For this example, I'm going to create another column that shows how many babies were born, then two fields to show the total babies and average babies born.

To get the total number, go to the cell and type "=sum(". Google will probably highlight what it thinks you want automatically, but if it doesn't, then just highlight the cells you want to add up and then hit Enter/Return:

Year	Babies Born
1900	33
1901	100
1902	4
1903	22
1904	21
1905	99
1906	73
1907	9
1908	9
1909	60
1910	81

Babies Born	=SUM
Average	SUM(B2:B12)
	Suggested based on the data.

The same method is used for averages, but you type =average(instead of sum:

Year	Babies Born
1900	33
1901	100
1902	4
1903	22
1904	21
1905	99
1906	73
1907	9
1908	9
1909	60
1910	81

Babies Born	46.45454545 ×
Average	=Average(B2:B12)

In seconds, we now know the number of babies born as well as the average for all years:

Year	Babies Born
1900	33
1901	100
1902	4
1903	22
1904	21
1905	99
1906	73
1907	9
1908	9
1909	60
1910	81
Babies Born	511
Average	46.45454545

Not happy with how it looks? You can apply basic formatting the same way you would in a Google Doc or Word Doc:

Year	Babies Born
1900	33
1901	100
1902	4
1903	22
1904	21
1905	
1906	73
1907	9
1908	9
1909	60
1910	81
Babies Born	412
Average	41.2

[3]

BEYOND THE BASICS

This chapter will cover:
- Creating charts
- Functions
- Scripts

Creating a Chart

People are visual. Numbers aren't very sexy. You need visuals to make them pop.

Before we go deeper into the fun world of functions, let's take the fun out of functions and do something fun: a chart.

I'll take the example above and create a chart that shows the babies born per year a little more visually.

To get started, I'll highlight what I want to show; in my example, only the top portion—the chart doesn't need to show the totals or averages:

	A	B
1	Year	Babies Born
2	1900	33
3	1901	100
4	1902	4
5	1903	22
6	1904	21
7	1905	99
8	1906	73
9	1907	9
10	1908	9
11	1909	60
12	1910	81
13		
14		
15	Babies Born	511
16	Average	46.45454545

Next, go to the toolbar and click the chart icon:

And just like that, we have a pretty line graph that represents our data:

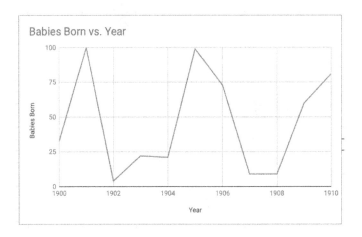

I know, I know...you're sitting there thinking: Lines! I hate lines!

Don't fret! You use the chart editor that opens a chart library to create dozens of other charts:

If you got so excited when the chart came up on your screen that you accidentally closed the chart editor, then just double click the chart and it will open back up:

You can use this editor to change the range (you add some more rows, for example, and want them represented) or reverse the data shown—you want to show the years on the lines, not the number of babies born.

Google has its own idea of what is pretty. It's probably different from yours. You don't want a blue line! You want a red line! You hate the black text! You want green! If there's one thing

Spreadsheet people are known for, it's their incredible talent for making numbers look sexy. Don't worry! You can customize almost everything here.

If you need to bring sexy back to your chart, then just go into your editor and select "Customize" right next to "Setup."

Setup   Customize

From here you can go section-to-section and change colors, fonts, and more:

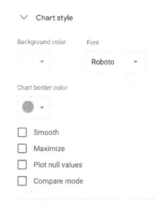

You can also change gridlines around on the bottom:

∨ Gridlines

Vertical axis   ▼

Major gridline count   Major gridline color

| Auto ▼ | ◯ Auto ▼ |

Minor gridline count   Minor gridline color

| None ▼ | Auto ▼ |

By default, Google will just stick the chart inconveniently over your data. If you click on it, you'll see a bunch of little blue boxes. That means you can either resize it (click on one and drag in/out to make it larger/smaller) or move it:

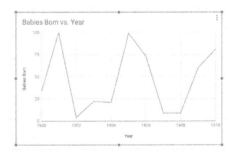

You'll also notice three little boxes in the upper right corner of the chart. That's your chart menu. Click that and you'll see several options:

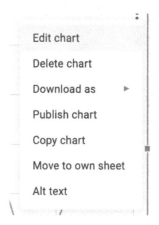

Edit chart

Delete chart

Download as ▶

Publish chart

Copy chart

Move to own sheet

Alt text

Download as is helpful if you want to insert it into emails as attachments or presentations. You can download it as an image or PDF.

You can also copy and paste the chart into other Google app—like Google Slides or Google Docs. Just click it and do CTRL+C on your keyboard to copy it, and CTRL+V to paste it.

Functionally Yours

Now that we had some fun, let's get serious and learn about functions.

What is a function exactly? Well, we already learned about two: Sum and Average. Functions are the formulas you put into cells to tell Google to calculate an equation.

There are a lot of functions. Go to your toolbar and click the function key, and you can see what I mean!

The main ones you use will be right at the top, which is helpful; below that, Google has categorized additional ones.

Because this book is meant to get you started quickly and not teach you all the features that you will never use, I won't cover every single function here. The goal is to show you how they work, so if there's one not covered here that you want to use, you'll know how.

I recommend you spend a few minutes looking at the list above and see if there's something that would be useful to what you are doing. There are hundreds of functions.

To use any of the functions in this list, go to the cell you want to show the equation in, and then click the function option and select the one you want to do; from here, select your data range. Once it's selected, hit return/enter.

If you decide later that you need to edit the function, go to the upper left corner—just under the tool bar. See the fx? When you select a cell with a function, it will show up here. Click in there, and then update the range that you want.

That's also the same place you go to edit any-thing in a cell—function or no function.

So Many Functions...That I Don't Want

Google Sheets has a lot of functions. It's over-whelming, but it doesn't have everything. If you be-come a power spreadsheets user, you might find it would be helpful to do something that there is no function for.

That doesn't mean you can't do it. It's just a lit-tle more involved. There are many more things you can do by creating a script. Scripts let you basically program your own function.

Scripts can be found by going to Tools > Scripts Editor.

This is going to launch a separate Google app for creating a script:

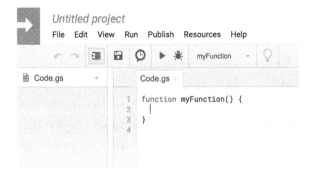

Below is an example of what a script might look like:

```
var ss = SpreadsheetApp.getActiveSpreadsheet();
var sheet = ss.getSheets()[0];

// The size of the two-dimensional array must match the size of
var values = [
    [ "2.000", "1,000,000", "$2.99" ]
];

var range = sheet.getRange("B2:D2");
range.setValues(values);
```

Once you have your script written, go to Publish > Deploy as Sheets add-on:

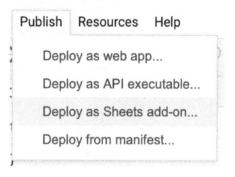

The topic of scripts is much too complicated for this book, but there are plenty of resources both in the Scripts app and online if this is an arena you'd like to dig deeper into later.

[4]

SHARING IS CARING

This chapter will cover:
- Sharing your sheet
- Editing and collaborating sheets
- Protecting sheets
- Data validation

Sharing Your Sheet

Now that you know your way around, you're ready for feedback from others.

If you know how to share a Google Doc, then you are in luck! Sharing Sheets is the same. Need a refresher?

Look up in the upper right corner. See the blue button that says Share? Click on that. It's going to open up several different sharing options.

When you click on that, a share box opens up, and you get a bunch of different options.

There's a few ways to share it:
1. Type their email address and let Google do the rest.
2. Manually (covered below).

When you email someone, you can also manage exactly what they can do. Click that little pencil icon. By default, it will say they can edit the doc. You can change it so they can only comment on the doc, or they can only view the doc:

You can also hit advance at the bottom of the share menu, and have a few more features—such as disabling print:

But let's say you don't want to email the first man. Let's say you just want to give him a link—that way he doesn't need to use his Google account to open it. To do that, follow the steps above, but in the upper corner of the box, click "Get shareable link."

Get shareable link 🔗

Once you click that, it will give you a sharable link—it even copies the link so if you hit CTRL-V (or right-click paste) you can paste that link anywhere you want.

If you click on can view, it will give you a drop-down menu with more features. It looks sort of like the other drop-down menu above, but there's an option that says "more."

Anyone with the link **can view** ▾

OFF - only specific people can access

Anyone with the link **can edit**

Anyone with the link **can comment**

✓ Anyone with the link **can view**

More...

When you click on "More," it gives you a few extra features—such as making the document public in search engines so anyone can find it.

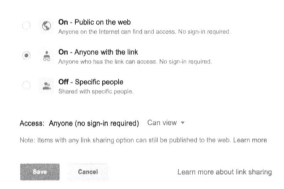

You can turn sharing off at any time, by hitting the "Share" button; once it's turned off, anyone who goes to that link—even if they've been there before—won't be able to see it. If you've emailed a person, they are still a viewer until you remove them.

If you have a person who really hates Google Sheets and refuses to view your document in anything but Word, Google Docs allows you to export your work to a Excel Document so you don't have to do all of the copying and font processing yourself. Just click on file --> download as --> Excel; there's a whole host of other exports here as well.

Editing and Collaborating With Others

The easiest way to make comments in a spreadsheet is to right-click and select Comment.

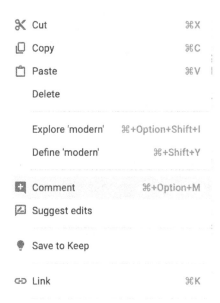

✂ Cut	⌘X
🗐 Copy	⌘C
📋 Paste	⌘V
Delete	
Explore 'modern'	⌘+Option+Shift+I
Define 'modern'	⌘+Shift+Y
➕ Comment	⌘+Option+M
🗂 Suggest edits	
💡 Save to Keep	
🔗 Link	⌘K

You can also get this, by selecting Insert on the toolbar, and Comment.

Either of these will bring up the comment box. Add your comment, and select the blue comment box when you are ready to post it. When you add a comment (or make a change), it's in real-time; that means if the person who is collaborating with you has the document open, they can actually watch you make the edits and add the comments.

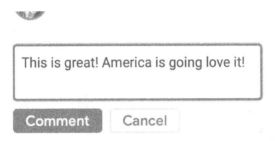

If you have multiple people working on the doc, you can type "@" and see a list of people you can mention; if you mention them, Google will notify them so they can add a reply to your comment.

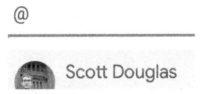

Once the comments in, it will show up on the side of Google Sheets.

ph

our

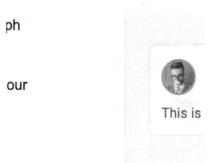

This is

You can delete or edit the comment, by click on those three little dots on the side of the box.

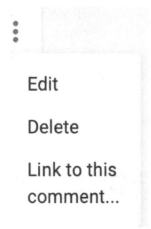

Edit

Delete

Link to this comment...

The person on the other end will be able to resolve the comment (that makes it disappear, but they can undo it)

Or they can reply to it.

To see all the versions of a document, go to file and see versions.

If there's going to be a lot of versions, then one suggestion is to name each one—which you can do here.

When you click See version history, you'll get a list of all the versions. Clicking on anyone will bring up that version. You can view it, or even restore it.

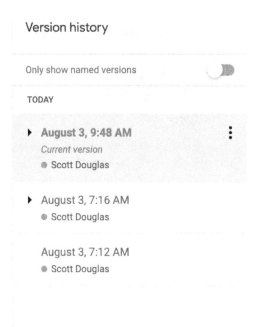

To get back to the document, just hit the back button in the menu (not the browser back button).

← **Today, 9:48 AM**

Protect a Spreadsheet

Google Sheets has an extra layer of protection not seen in Google Docs. To apply it, go to Tools > Protect Sheet.

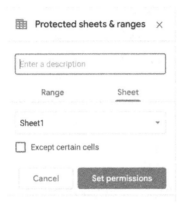

From here you can do several things:

Give it a description – Why does it need a description? Because you can create several difference protections.

Select the range.

Set permissions – you can, for example, give one person the ability to make changes and another the ability only to see it.

Data Validation

Let's say you give someone permission to edit the sheet and they add in something wrong; that error messes up the entire spreadsheet! Now what? Spent hours trying to figure out the mess they made, right?

Sure, why not! But why don't we make sure they don't make that mess to begin with!

Data validation let's you add in rules so people can't add in things incorrectly. For example, let's say someone doesn't know the answer so they just put in "?" or "N/A." You can set up a rule that forces them only to use a number.

To add one in, highlight the cells you want to apply it to and then go to Data > Data validation. This brings up the option box.

From here you need to set your rule (or criteria).

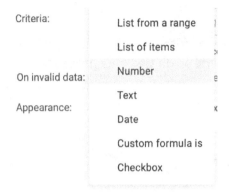

My rule is the data here needs to be a number between 0 and 101. If you want to get really fancy, you can add in a custom formula.

Next, you need to say what happens if they break the rule. Do you want to outright reject it or just give them a warning. In my case, I'm all about rejection. But I'm a nice guy too, so I'm going to tell them why I'm rejecting them.

Now if someone tries to add anything but a number, then tell get this message.

There was a problem

Numbers Only!

OK

[5]

THIS AND THAT

This chapter will cover:
- Surveys
- Google Sheets menus

Survey's Into Data

One area Google Sheets has Excel and other programs beat is it's survey integration.

Using Google Forms to create a survey, you can have all the answers go right into a Google Sheet so you can collate your results.

To get started go to Insert > Forms.

This is going to launch a separate tab with the Google Forms application.

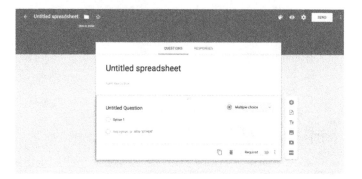

I'm going to make this survey simple, but if you want to jazz it up, there's all kinds of options for adding photos and changing styles around. Use the menu on the right side for those options.

For my survey, I'm going to make it a drop-down survey. You can change the question type by selecting the drop down to the right side of the question name; you can have as many types as you want in the survey—for example, question one could be multiple choice and question two could be a drop down.

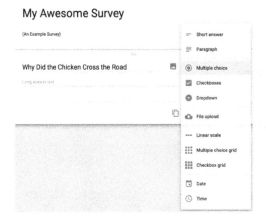

This changes our answers to editable fields. Right now, it has room for two questions. As soon as I stop typing in the second answer, a slot will be added for a third question.

More answer slots are added with each question.

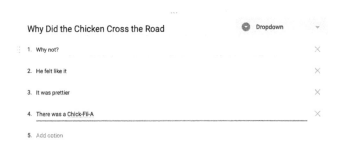

When you are done, click the "Send Form" button in the upper right corner:

I don't want to send the form to anyone—I want it to be a link. So, I'm going to click the link icon next to the email one (it's the middle one).

When someone goes to my survey, it will look a little bit different from the one that was in the editor because all the menu fields are gone.

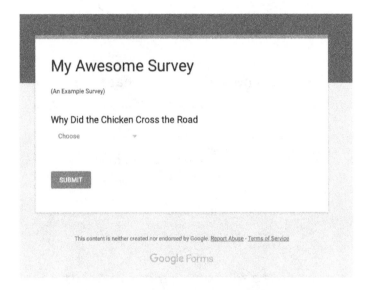

Once they click submit, they'll see a confirmation. You can make this a custom confirmation or use the default Google one.

Now that you have a response, go back to your Sheet and you'll see a new tab has been added on the bottom of the sheet for form responses.

Click that and you can see what the person answered.

	A	B	C
1	Timestamp	Why Did the Chicken Cross the Road	
2	8/5/2019 12:30:48	He felt like it	
3			
4			
5			
6			

If you need to make changes to it, just go to Form from your menu bar.

Form Add-ons Help   All changes ;

    Edit form

    Send form

    Go to live form

    Embed form in a webpage

    Show summary of responses

    Unlink form

If you have multiple forms, then this option will not show on your menu bar unless you are inside that form tab. So if you don't see the option, then click the tab for the Form responses and then it will appear in the menu.

If you decide to delete the form, it's a little different from a normal tab. A normal tab, you right-click on the tab and hit delete, it will tell you that you can't. You have to unlink it first. How? Easy!

Right-click on the form tab you want to unlink and select Unlink form.

Once it's unlinked, you'll be able to delete it, by right-clicking and selecting delete.

This and That

By now, you should be have a really good idea how Google Sheets work. Before leaving you, I'll cover a few more features that you should know about.

By default, Google will base the Sheet on your Google Account; if your Google Account thinks you live in Spain, then that's how the Sheet is set up.

You can change this by going to File > Spreadsheet settings.

Spreadsheet settings

This is helpful if you, for example, live in the United States, but happen to be working on a Sheet for someone who lives in the UK. You can change the settings, so it shows as pounds instead of dollars.

Settings for this spreadsheet   ×

General   Calculation

Locale

United States ▾   This affects formatting details such as functions, dates, and
                          currency.

Time zone

(GMT-08:00) Pacific Time ▾   Your spreadsheet's history will be recorded in this time zone. This
                             will affect all time-related functions.

Display language: English

                                        Cancel   Save settings

When you start working on large documents, it gets difficult to find things. Imagine you have 100,000 cells and you have to find the one with the number "12a?b44." Good luck with that! Fortunately for you, there's something called "Find and Replace" under the Edit menu.

Edit	View	Insert	Format	Data	To
↰ Undo				⌘Z	
↱ Redo				⌘Y	
✂ Cut				⌘X	
▢ Copy				⌘C	
▯ Paste				⌘V	
Paste special				▸	
Find and replace				⌘+Shift+H	

Not only does it find the cell you are looking for, but it let's you replace it with something else. For example, I can tell it to find every example of "California" and replace it with "CA."

Another handy feature if you have lots of rows is the freeze option. That's under View > Freeze.

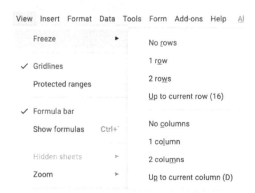

What exactly is freeze? Typically, you have a top row that is sort of like a menu. It tells the view what is in each column. And then you have the first column that has something else descriptive—such as dates. Now imagine you have 10,000 rows. You're on row 2079, column AA. You can't remember what that row stands for. If you had freeze row enabled, then that top menu (or side column) would be frozen, so no matter where you are, you always see it.

If you are editing a lot of formulas, go to View and check off "Show formulas." This will show you the formula instead of the answer. It's helpful for editing formulas.

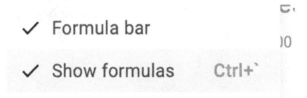

If you are in the middle of a large sheet and need to add in a row in the middle, then select the row you want to add it to, then go to Insert > and select Row above, Row below, or anywhere else you want it.

Insert Format Data Tools For

Row **above**

Row **below**

Column **left**

Column **right**

Cells and shift **down**

Cells and shift **right**

Insert > Checkbox is useful if you have people viewing it and you want them to confirm that they see something.

 Checkbox

If you want to add a new tab to the bottom of your sheet, you can either click the + in the lower left corner of the sheet, or go to Insert > New sheet. To delete the sheet, right-click the tab and select delete.

New sheet	Shift+F11

You learned earlier about setting rules to a Sheet with data validation. You can do something similar with format. This is found in Format > Conditional formatting.

Conditional formatting

With conditional formatting, you can, for example, tell the sheet if the cell is empty, it's green, but if it has content, then it's blue. You can do it for run cell, or highlight multiple cells to do it for several.

Conditional format rules   ✕

Single color   Color scale

Apply to range

A1   ⊞

Format rules

Format cells if...

Is not empty   ▾

Formatting style

Default

B   *I*   U   S   A ▾   ◇ ▾

Cancel   Done

+ Add another rule

If you are working with a large sheet, and want to make sure there's no duplicate content, then highlight the range, then select Data > Remove duplicates. This will go through the range and remove anything that's the same.

Remove duplicates New

Macros are a bit complex, they help you create sequences to automate certain tasks. I won't cover them here, but if you want to use them, it's under Tools > Macro.

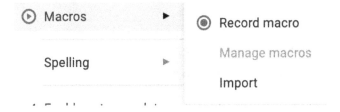

Also under tools is Notification rules.

Notification rules

This is what you will use if you want to be notification when someone edits your document, or adds something to your survey. You can either be emailed immediately or once a day.

Set notification rules   Help   ✕

Notify me at roboscott@gmail.com when...

○ Any changes are made
○ A user submits a form

Notify me with...

○ Email - daily digest
○ Email - right away

                          Cancel   Save

There's still a lot to learn, but I hope you now have the understanding and using Sheets comfortably.

If you find yourself copying a lot of formulas and getting errors, try pasting only the values. That means it will only copy the number and not the actual formula. You can do this by pressing CTRL+Shift+V, or by going to Edit > Paste special.

[6]

GOOGLE SHEETS KEYBOARD SHORTCUTS

You can see all the keyboard shortcuts in Google Sheets by selecting Help > Keyboard shortcuts.

For your reference, below are some of the most common ones you'll use.

Common actions

Select column	Ctrl + Space
Select row	Shift + Space
Select all	Ctrl + a
Undo	Ctrl + z
Redo	Ctrl + y
Find	Ctrl + f
Find and replace	Ctrl + h

Fill range	Ctrl + Enter
Fill down	Ctrl + d
Fill right	Ctrl + r
Copy	Ctrl + c
Cut	Ctrl + x
Paste	Ctrl + v
Paste values only	Ctrl + Shift + v

Format cells

Bold	Ctrl + b
Underline	Ctrl + u
Italic	Ctrl + i
Strikethrough	Alt + Shift + 5
Center align	Ctrl + Shift + e
Left align	Ctrl + Shift + l
Right align	Ctrl + Shift + r
Apply top border	Alt + Shift + 1
Apply right border	Alt + Shift + 2
Apply bottom border	Alt + Shift + 3
Apply left border	Alt + Shift + 4
Remove borders	Alt + Shift + 6
Apply outer border	Alt + Shift + 7
Insert link	Ctrl + k
Insert time	Ctrl + Shift + ;
Insert date	Ctrl + ;
Insert date and time	Ctrl + Alt + Shift + ;
Format as decimal	Ctrl + Shift + 1
Format as time	Ctrl + Shift + 2
Format as date	Ctrl + Shift + 3
Format as currency	Ctrl + Shift + 4
Format as percentage	Ctrl + Shift + 5
Format as exponent	Ctrl + Shift + 6

Clear formatting	Ctrl + \

Use formulas

Show all formulas	Ctrl + ~
Insert array formula	Ctrl + Shift + Enter
Collapse an expanded array for-mula	Ctrl + e
Show/hide formula help *(when entering a formula)*	Shift + F1
Full/compact formula help *(when entering a formula)*	F1
Absolute/relative references *(when entering a formula)*	F4
Toggle formula result previews *(when entering a formula)*	F9
Resize formula bar *(move up or down)*	Ctrl + Up / Ctrl + Down

PART 4: GOOGLE SLIDES

[1]

GOOGLE SLIDES CRASH COURSE

This chapter will cover:
- What is Slides?
- Slides crash course

How many times do you work on a presentation that you will get absolutely no feedback on and want no help?

Maybe you're the type that likes to whip something up and have no practice or feedback at all? Most of us are the former. Before we stand in front of a group of people, we want to make sure we're as polished as possible.

The problem is PowerPoint wasn't built like that. It was built as a desktop program that one person would use at a time.

Google realized the problem and seized the opportunity when they launched Google Slides over ten years ago.

Google Slides is a cloud-based presentation editor that can replace PowerPoint or Keynote.

If you'd like to get the most out of the software, then let's get started!

Slides Crash Course

There's a lot to cover. In the next section, we'll start from scratch with a blank presentation, but before we get there, I'm going to quickly go over the main tool bars.

This is going to be a quick overview, so if there's something you don't understand, that's okay—I'll cover it in more detail later in the book.

The first button is one you'll probably use a lot. That's how you add a new Slide. When you click the drop down, you can see all the predefined layouts. Click it and the layout will be added (hint: you'll be able to change it later).

Next to that is the undo, redo, and print icon. The last option is the format painter. This copies one style to another—for example, you want to copy the font color and size of one text, to another text. To use it, just highlight the style you want to copy, select the icon, then click the text you want to copy it to.

Next is the zoom icon. This lets you zoom in or out, so you can see more or less of your slide.

The insert options are next. The first icon (the cursor) lets you select an object, the next lets you add a text box, next to that is the insert image option, and finally, the last, insert a shape.

There's one final insert option: line. There are a couple different lines you can when you select the drop down. The scribble line is if you want to draw the line freehand.

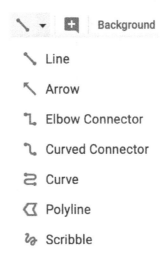

Because Google Slides is so collaborative, you'll probably use the next button a lot: the comment option. This lets you add comments to any slide or text.

The background button let's you add an image or color to your slide background.

Background

The layout option looks similar to the Add Slide button. This lets you change the layout of the selected slide.

The theme button is similar to layout, but instead of text, it's changing the style of the slide—adding a background image, for example.

Theme

Finally, the Transition button is where you tell Google Slides what to do whenever you go to the next slide.

Transition

Hanging out at the far right side is the menu hide button. Use this to toggle between hide and unhide.

⌃

Over on the far left side, the side menu has three options: calendar, Google keep, and tasks. These are sort of mini apps. They don't change your slide—they just help you keep notes and pull up dates.

[2]

GETTING STARTED WITH GOOGLE SLIDES

This chapter will cover:
- Creating your first slide
- The basics

Now that we know the basics, let's dig in and see how to use the features in practice. To get started, head to drive.google.com (create an account if you haven't already) and click the create new button, then Google Slides, and blank presentation.

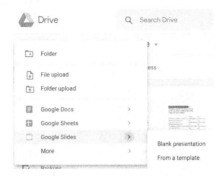

Right off the bat, it probably looks a little familiar to you if you've used PowerPoint or Keynote.

For this book, we're going to create a presentation on how to know if your friend is a monster. How many books on Google Slides, also give you valuable information on friendship?! Your welcome!

I find the best kind of learning is through actually doing something, so fill free to work on a similar presentation as you go.

First, things first: let's rename our document. Technically, this isn't required. You could give it no name and it's still going to be saving in the background. Naming it will just help you find it later.

To name it, just click once on that name area in the upper left corner and start typing. Hit enter when you are done.

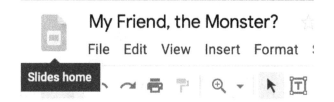

Want to rename it? Simple. Just click in that area again. Gone are the days of File > Save As.

Now let's move to our first slide—the title slide—and give the presentation a name.

The 9 Steps

To Know If Your Friend Is a Monster

That's pretty straightforward, but it's also a little...boring. Let's add a fun background to it.

For this book, I went to google.com/images. That's a nice resource for pictures, but you have to keep in mind that many are copyrighted, so be mindful of what you are using—especially if the presentation is for non-instructional commercial use.

Once you have your image, you can either save it, or just copy and paste it right into your slide.

To add it, there's two methods. I prefer the second, because there's more customation to it, but I'll show you both approaches here.

For the first approach, go to your toolbar and click the Background button. From here you can either give it a solid background color, or make an image a background.

Background   ×

Color   ▾

Image   Choose image

Reset to theme   Reset

              Add to theme   Done

If you are just using a color, then it can work. If you are using an image, then personally I find it problematic because there's not a lot of adjustments that can be made to the image at this level. Take a look at the background below.

Not incredibly easy to see the text, right? How do we fix that? We use the second option. Either copy and paste the image onto the slide or go to Insert > Slide. This will put the image on top of the text. Not much better right? You can fix that by right-clicking the image and selecting "Send to back."

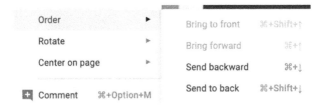

That basically makes it the same as having it as a background image, so it's still not where it needs to be. But now when you click on the image, it brings up a format menu. One option is transparency. Transparency makes the image more see through—like a watermark.

After making it a little transparent, it looks like the below image.

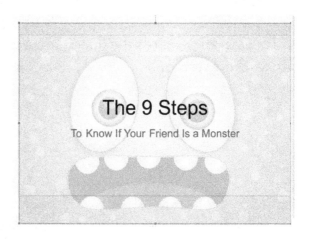

Better, right? But it is bigger than the slide. If you are presenting the slide, it will only show what's in the slide box, but it's much easier to work on a presentation in editor mode when it matches what the presentation will look like, so let's crop it. Right-click on the image, then select "Crop image."

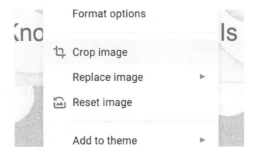

This brings up small blue boxes. Just drag those in so it fits in the slide.

Now we are ready for our next slide. There are two methods to do this. Click the + sign in the menu toolbar.

The second method is to click under the first slide and hit the enter / return button on your keyboard.

The default slide will look like the below.

You can change the layout by either right-clicking on the slide thumbnail on the left side. Or going to the menu and clicking on layout.

I'll change my layout to two columns.

Next, I'll add in some content.

> **There are two kinds of friends**
>
> Good friends   Bad friends

Awesome! Visually stunning! Let's call it a day! Don't get ahead of yourself, cowboy…there's still some work to be done here. Let's throw in some images. Again, you can either do Insert > Picture or just copy and paste it in.

Those pictures are a little…black and white—both literally and figuratively. Right-click on the image, then go format options. For this image, I'm going to check off "Reflection" to make it pop a little. This puts a shadow effect on the image.

The pictures are fine. Now let's work on the text. The header needs to be all caps. We can either type it again with all caps on, or we highlight the text, and then go to Format > Text > Capitalization > UPPERCASE.

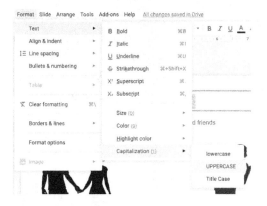

Do the same to the text under that, but for that make it Title Case. Next we want to center align it. You may not see this option if you have the format menu open, but it's still there. To the far right of the toolbar, you'll see three dots. Click that, and it will bring up the hidden menu. From here you can center align it.

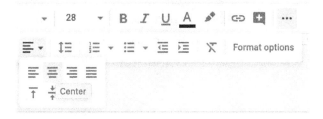

We are also going to change the text color using the button with the A and black line under it.

A

Now everything will be centered, and a different color.

That's still not very colorful. We could add an image to the background like the first slide, but images as backgrounds can make things look too busy. So let's do a solid color. Click Background from the toolbar and then change it to the one you want.

That's better. But I want the slide header to pop out more. I'm going to put a separate background behind it. Go to the Shapes button on the menu bar and select the rectangle.

Now drag a rectangle on the upper portion of that slide. I want the box itself to pop more, so I'm also going to right-click, select Format options, and check off "Drop shadow." This gives the box a more 3D effect by putting a subtle shadow behind it.

Now we just need to send the box to the back so the text is in front of it. To do that, right-click on the box and under Order select send to back. I also click the text and moved it a little higher up, so it was in the middle of the box.

Now the slide is taking shape, but let's do a few more things. Next, let's make the subtitle text come out more. Click the top box you just created and copy and paste it (CTRL+C and CTRL+V). Then move that box under the top one, right-click it, and do format options; change the color of the box so it's not the same as the other box.

THERE ARE TWO KINDS OF FRIENDS

After you change the color, right-click and select Order and send to the back. The text is kind of
small, so let's make it bigger and then adjust it so
it's more in the middle of the box. Change the font
size in the menu bar; by default it's 14.

Finally, that dark grey I used doesn't really
work. I'm going to make the box white. Right-click,
select format options, and then change the color to
white.

I want to put a line between friendship to separate the good friends from the bad. Go to the menu bar, click the line option, and select the first line. As you draw the line, hold the shift on the keyboard—that's going to make it a straight line—so it doesn't go diagonal at all.

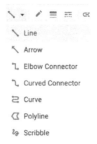

The line is going to be pretty thin; that works for some things, but here we want to beef it up. Click the line, then go to the menu bar. See the box with the lines of different weights? That's what you want. It's like a font size, but for a shape. If you don't see it, then you haven't selected the line. Click it one time.

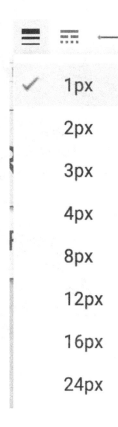

Now that the line is wider, we have everything where we want it to be.

You can create a different look for every slide, but to save yourself a lot of time, copying the slide is a lot faster. Go to the left pane where the slide thumbnails are. Right-click, and select, duplicate slides.

From here, all we have to do is take out the text we don't want and change the images.

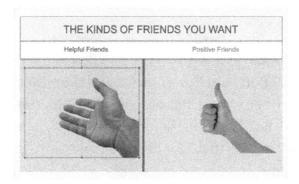

The image above feels a little off. I don't want both hands going the same direction. That's an easy fix. Select one of the images, select format options, and then under rotate, select Flip.

That's going to horizontally flip the image you've selected.

So things are going great! You have three slides! But wait! You just realized that the third slide needs to be the second slide! Now what! Easy! Just click the thumbnail of the slide in the left pane, and drag it to where you want it to go.

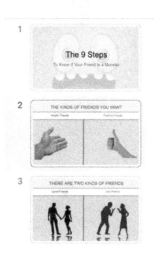

Now that you have the Slides, you need transitions between them. You won't see this in editor mode, but transitions is what happens when you are presenting a presentation between each slide—does it show a dissolve, for example.

To add in a transition, right-click on the thumbnail you want, and then select change transition.

This brings up the Transition menu; you can change one transition or apply the transition to all of the slides.

[3]

SHARING IS CARING

This chapter will cover:
- How to share
- Sharing settings
- Naming versions

Are you ready to share your slides about friends with your friends? Google Slides is a collaborative platform, so sharing is where things really come together. With sharing you can get feedback and also have others edit your slides (or you can disable editing and only get feedback)

To share, click the Share button in the upper right corner.

If you've used any other Google apps software, then you'll probably know what to do next—they all work exactly the same. You'll have a box to either share the Slide with specific people via email, or you can send them a link to it.

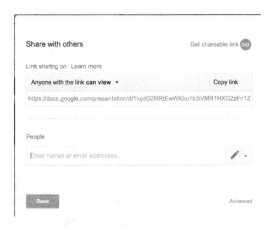

If you click on can view you'll get a drop down with varies options. If you only want people to see it, but not do anything else, for example.

If you click on Advanced, you'll have even more options—such as preventing editors from adding people or disabling copying anything in the doc.

Once people are in your document, and ready to make changes, things get a little—difficult. Unlike Google Docs where you can track changes, Google Slides doesn't have that option. If someone makes a change, there's no good visible way to see it.

You can ask them to comment instead. To do that, have them right-click and select comment. Or go to Insert > Comment:

There's one final way to keep track of changes—albeit, not the ideal one. That way is to view the history. You can see the history by going to File > Version history > See version history.

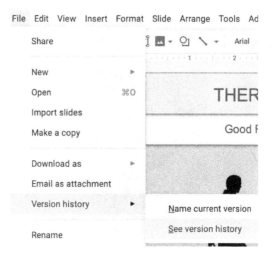

This will show you a list of changes and timestamp when they were made.

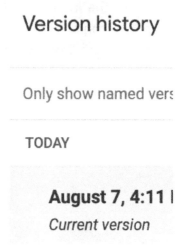

If you are using this method, then my advice is to have people go in after a change and name the version: File > Version history > Name current version.

If you have someone whose old fashion—like PowerPoint, old fashion—you can also export it and email it to them. This is under File > Download as. There's all kinds of options.

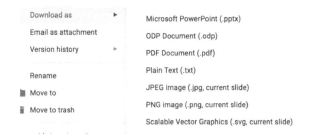

If you are giving a presentation, my advice is to export it as a PowerPoint and PDF. This way if you are ever presenting somewhere and you show up and they say, "Oh, we don't have Internet in this room—and you'll be using a computer without PowerPoint" You'll have something to display.

[4]

PRESENTING YOUR BIG IDEA!

This chapter will cover:
- Presenting to others
- Speaker notes
- Audience questions

So speaking of that big presentation, now what?! That's the easy part. See that big Present button in the right corner? Guess what that does?!

But there's more to presenting then, presenting! Click that arrow next to Present, and you'll see a few more options.

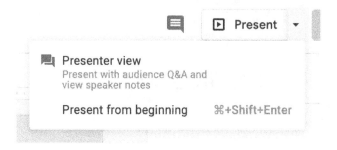

One is Presenter view, which I'll cover in just a few minutes. When your presentation is open, there's a new menu. In this menu you'll be able to turn on Q & A and notes, which will be covered below, and use the pointer. Pointer is kind of like a laser pointer; if you are doing mouse movements, then this will make it easier for viewers to watch themovements.

Using Presenter mode

By now, you've probably noticed there's a little box on the bottom that says "Click to add speaker notes." Want to take a wild guess and say what that is for? If you guessed, "Speaker notes" then congratulations, you can read!

You can actually make that area bigger or non-existent by clicking on those three dots in the middle and making it go up or down. For the sake of this book, we'll keep them right where they are.

Okay, so what are speaker notes? This is what appears on your screen when you are presenting a presentation. What do I mean by "your screen"? When you give a presentation, you usually will have your laptop connected to either a projector or TV, right? So your screen would be the laptop, and the other screen would be what it's connected to.

Speaker notes is kind of like having paper notes in front of you. It can be whatever you want. Since the audience doesn't see them, it doesn't matter—whatever is helpful when you are giving the presentation.

I'm going to be speakinging here today about friends and why you don't have any! [pause for awkward laugher]

You could technically set it up to mirror your screen, but having a presenter screen is very useful. In speaker mode, you'll see the notes, the amount of time that has passed, and thumbnail of the slide coming up next, and the ability to get audience questions.

If the notes are too small for you, then you can use the "- | +" buttons to make them bigger.

ng here today about
t have any! [pause

What's really cool about presenting in Google Slides is the audience can ask questions. To accept questions while you present, you just have to turn it on. Next to speaker notes, click Audience Tools, then click the Start Now button.

There's a toggle to turn it on and off, and a link to send people.

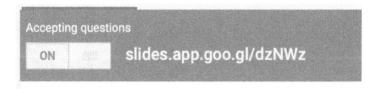

When the person goes to that link, they are presented with a forum to ask ask their questions. They can either do it as a person or anonymously.

Other people will see it and they can upvote it or downvote it. That helps push up or down questions; a question with a 20 upvotes will be hire in the question que then a question with 2.

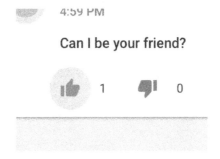

On the presenter version, they will see the question, the number of upvotes, and have an option to present it.

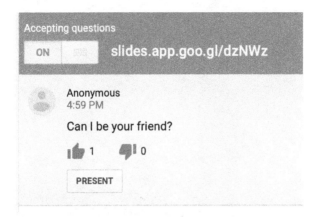

If the presenter hits the Present button, it will replace the presentation with the question.

To return to your slide, present the present button below the question again.

[5]

BEYOND THE BASICS

This chapter will cover:
- Importing and creating charts
- Creating diagrams
- Adding videos

Importing Charts from Google Sheets

Collaboration is Google Slides standout feature, as you probably can tell; something else that really makes it shine, however, is the way it interacts with other Google apps. Everything is connected through the cloud, which makes integration a breeze.

To illustrate this point, we are going to import a chart created in Google Sheets into Slides.

Start off by creating a new Slide. I'll make one simple and call it The Friendly Chart.

The Friendly Chart

Now we need are chart. Open up Google Sheets, and create a basic chart. It's simple to do. Just create two columns. One with labels or names and one with data.

B	C
December 1	57
November 30	18
November 16	22
December 9	265
December 31	3.5
December 26	350
October 20	315
October 30	4
Septembe4 23	24
September 29	5
November 23	32
October 10	5
November 18	12

Next, highlight the area you are going to make a chart of, and go to Insert > Chart.

Insert   Format   Data   Tools   Add-

13 Rows **above**

13 Rows **below**

2 Columns **left**

2 Columns **right**

Cells and shift **down**

Cells and shift **right**

Chart

Your chart is added right into your Sheet.

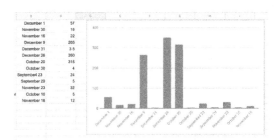

From here, click the chart and do CTRL C, which will copy it. Now go back into Google Slide, select the slide you want to add it to, and on your keyboard, hit CTRL V. This is going to ask you if you want it linked or unlinked.

Linked will connect the app to the spreadsheet, so if you update data, it will update here as well; unlinked makes it like a static image that will never change. For this example, we are doing "Link to spreadsheet."

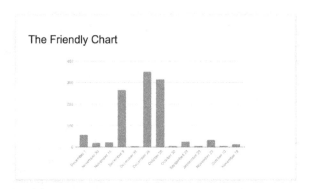

Now that it's added in, you can click on the upper right corner of the chart and have a few options. If you pick Unlink, then you will not be able to link it back, so think carefully here. Open source will let you go back in and edit the data.

When you go back into your spreadsheet and edit the data, it will change the chart in real-time. You don't have to create a new chart.

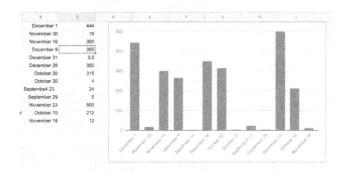

Now that it's changed in the Sheet, it will have a new option when you return to slides. Click the chart in slides. See the Update button?

Click that and it will update the chart to match what's the updated data.

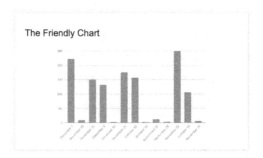

Now that you've entered a caption, go ahead and open up Google Spreadsheets. We're about to do the exact same thing we did when we inserted the chart into our Google Doc. Save the chart as an image on your hard drive, and then upload it into your presentation.

If you don't have a chart and want to do it from scratch, you can also go to Insert > Chart.

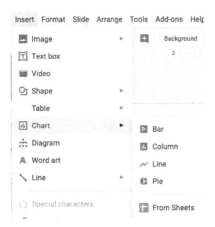

When you insert a chart from here, you will be creating a spreadsheet that's tied to the chart. It's going to add in a dummy chart; from here, you will click the menu button in the upper right corner of the dummy chart, then select "Open source."

Creating Diagrams

Diagrams aren't as common as charts, but are very resourceful when creating things like pricing tables and timelines.

To get started, create a new slide, and then go to Insert > Timeline.

What's nice about diagrams, is the hard part is already done. Google has several prebuilt templates and all you have to do is customize them a little. To start with, you'll see several different types of diagrams you can work with.

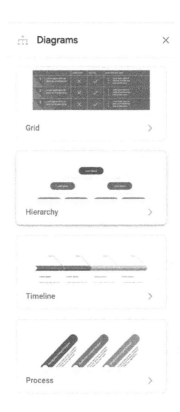

Depending on the type you select, you'll next be able to select how many dates you want to show and the color that will be used. As you update these two fields, you'll notice the preview thumbnails changing in real-time. Once you get this portion customized, select the type of diagram you want to use.

The diagram is added into your slide, and from here you can customize it to whatever suits your needs.

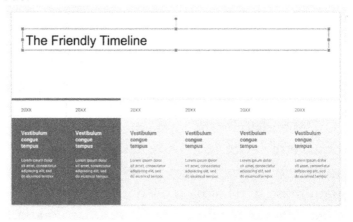

Adding Video to a Presentation

There's another app integration you can use with Google Slides. Unless you just spent the past ten years living under a rock, you've probably heard of it: YouTube.

When you add a video to Slides, you can either add a YouTube video or add one from your Google Drive. Both are easy to do, but there's a caveat here: both are online. That means if there's no Internet where you are presenting, that videos not going to load.

To get started, add another Slide, and then go to Insert > Video.

The first thing you'll see is a search bar to find your video on YouTube. That's the easiest option—especially if you don't already have a video and want to use something already created.

If you have a video on YouTube, then you can use the "By URL" option to copy in the link—this is only YouTube links, so if that video is on something like Vimeo, then you are out of luck. The last option is Google Drive. If you have a video in Google Drive, select this. Unlike photos, where if you don't have it upload it, then you can upload it directly, videos is a bit more cumbersome. You have to upload it to Google Drive, then come back and find it here. It's not complicated, but the extra step makes it a little less user friendly.

Once the video is added, right-click and select video options. This will bring up a menu with several options. The one you'll want to pay the most attention to is Format options. Under format options, you can select when the video will start and end, which is great if you only plan on showing a short clip.

You can also check off autoplay when presenting. When this is selected, the video will start as soon as you get to the slide. It can work for some videos, but if you haven't practiced the timing of your presentation, it could make for an awkward transition. If you don't check it off, then you start the video by pressing the play button.

[6]

THIS AND THAT

This chapter will cover:
- Overview of Slides menus
- Finding and using templates

The goal of this book is to get you up and running quickly; it's not to give you a comprehensive look at every feature—even the ones you will probably never used.

Before leaving you, however, I'll give you a high-level overview of some of the features not covered. Some are self-explanatory, so I'll move quick.

The view menu is what you see on the screen—do you want to see the presentation? The outline? Speaker notes? This is where you change it.

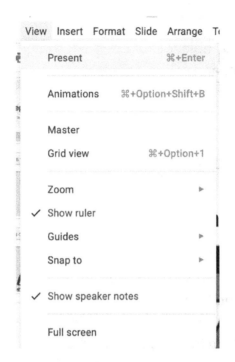

Some of the less obvious views:

Animations – we didn't cover animations in the book. Animations isn't exactly what it sounds. It's not a cartoon dancing across the screen. Think of animations like slide transitions, but for objects. So you can have the slide start, and then say "on click, I want this object to dissolve in." It's a resourceful feature, but too many animations can also make a presentation feel gimmicky, so be careful. If you want to add an animation, right-click on the image or object (object could be text) that you want to animate, and select Animate.

The animate view let's you see all of your animations, and also edit each one.

Grid view simply lays out all of your slides in a grid. It's helpful if you have dozens of slides and need to organize or print them, but not useful for shorter presentations.

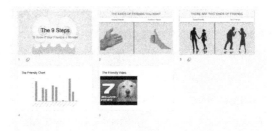

Guides will turn on rulers and is useful if you need to add in something with more precision.

We've covered most of the features in the insert menu.

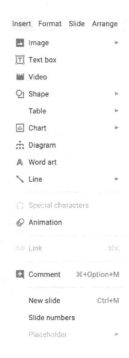

Some of the ones not covered:
- Word Art – If you've used Word, then you might be familiar with this; it makes text pop a little more by giving them a more 3D feel.
- Slide numbers – page numbers, but for slides.

Both the View and Slides menu have something called "master"; in the Slides menu it's "edit master."

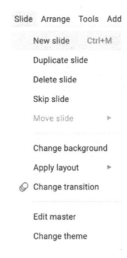

What the heck is master? It's a very technical area of slides that probably 90% of users never step foot in, but it's still good to know. This is where you can change how styles look. For example, you want to say "whenever I use a heading 1, I want it to be 30 in size, not 16." It saves you a lot of time if you are working on several presentations.

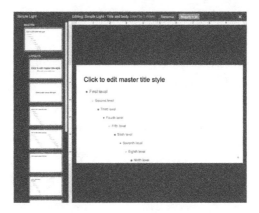

Spell checker and dictionary are found in the tools menu; that's what most people go to that menu for. If you are doing a Q & A, it's helpful to note there is a history option here. If you already gave the presentation, this is where you would go to review all the questions.

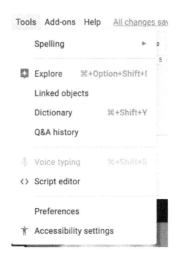

There are a lot of third party apps. This can be found in the "Add-ons menu."

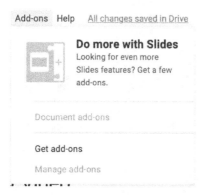

Finally, the help menu is obviously where you go for help, but there's also trainings here. These are free and very useful when you have time to learn more.

Custom Presentations from Templates

You'll recall when you first started that you could add a blank presentation or start from a template. We did blank to get started. Once you know your way around Slides, adding from a Template could save you a lot of time.

To add a template, go to your Google Drive, and select New > Google Slides > Start from a template.

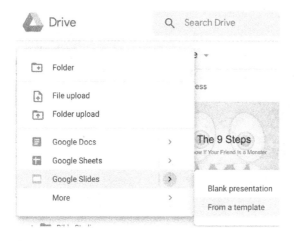

This brings up a template gallery of dozens of different presentations. The idea here is to find a style you like and then add in your own version.

Don't let the names fool you. Just because it says it's a wedding template, for example, doesn't mean it's not ideal for business.

Once you select one, you'll notice right away that several slides have already been added in.

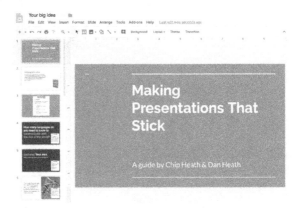

Nothing about these templates are locked in. What do I mean by that? You can change literally everything about them—images, color backgrounds, font sizes, text boxes. Now that you know your way around Slides, you'll have no problem customizing them to fit your needs.

The template gallery is nice. There's a lot there. But it's not comprehensive. I recommend browsing it, but when you are out of ideas, then go to the place with millions of ideas: Google.

Start by Googling "google slides templates."

There are only 55,000,000 results, so you'll have no problem sorting through that in no time!

In all seriousness, I do recommend browsing through some of the top matches, but I also recommend making the search specific to your industry. Such as "google slides templates for education."

People use slides for more than presentations. You can create books with it, resumes, portfolios—it's a powerful tool, so don't be afraid to think outside the box.

Once you see something you like, then download it, and then upload it to your Google Drive as a file.

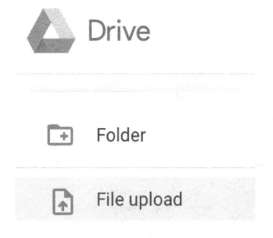

From here just right-click on the file once it's uploaded and open it as a Slide.

[7]

GOOGLE SLIDES KEYBOARD SHORTCUTS

You can see all the keyboard shortcuts in Google Slides by selecting Help > Keyboard shortcuts.

For your reference, below are some of the most common ones you'll use.

Common actions	
New slide	**Ctrl + m**
Duplicate slide	**Ctrl + d**
Undo	**Ctrl + z**
Redo	**Ctrl + y**
	Ctrl + Shift + z
Copy	**Ctrl + c**
Cut	**Ctrl + x**
Paste	**Ctrl + v**

Insert or edit link	**Ctrl + k**
Open link	**Alt + Enter**
Delete	**Delete**
Select all	**Ctrl + a**
Find	**Ctrl + f**
Find and replace	**Ctrl + h**
Open...	**Ctrl + o**
Print	**Ctrl + p**
Turn on captions while presenting	**Ctrl + Shift + c**
Text	
Bold	**Ctrl + b**
Italic	**Ctrl + i**
Underline	**Ctrl + u**
Subscript	**Ctrl + ,**
Superscript	**Ctrl + .**
Strikethrough	**Alt + Shift + 5**
Clear formatting	**Ctrl + **
	Ctrl + Space
Left align	**Ctrl + Shift + l**
Right align	**Ctrl + Shift + r**
Center align	**Ctrl + Shift + e**
Justify	**Ctrl + Shift + j**
Presenting	
Stop presenting	**Esc**
Next	→
Previous	←
Go to specific slide (7 followed by Enter goes to slide 7)	**Number followed by Enter**
First slide	**Home**
Last slide	**End**
Open speaker notes	**s**

Open audience tools	**a**
Toggle laser pointer	**l**
Print	**Ctrl + p**
Toggle captions (English only)	**Ctrl + Shift + c**
Toggle full screen	**F11**
Video Player	
Toggle play/pause	**k**
Rewind 10 seconds	**u**
Fast forward 10 seconds	**o**

PART 5: GOOGLE FORMS

[1]

GOOGLE FORMS AND LESSER USED GOOGLE APPS

This chapter will cover:
- Using Google Forms
- Overview of Google Drawing, Google Map, Google Sites, Google Jamboard

Google Forms

If you click that "More" option when you are creating a new document, one very handy application you'll see is "Google Forms."

Google Forms lets you create custom surveys. It's very simple and resourceful. Once you click on a blank form to get started, you see a screen like this:

The first question is already there. You just have to name everything—the name of the form, and what the question is. By default, it's multiple choice, but if you click the multiple-choice dropdown, you'll get several other options:

To add a new question, just click the "+" on the side menu:

It will add the question under the previous, but you can change its position by clicking the six small boxes to drag it above (or if there's multiple questions, below).

⋮⋮⋮

You can also use that side menu, to add links, text, images, YouTube videos, and sections.

When you are done with your form and you want to share it, click the send button:

This will bring up a box that lets you specify how you will share it: by email, link, or embedded on a webpage:

To toggle between each, just click the icon that represents how you want to see it. The middle, for example (seen below), is by link; the < > is to embed in a webpage.

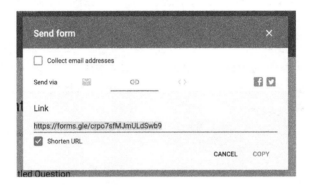

When you embed into a webpage, you'll be able to customize the size:

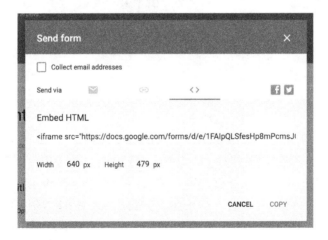

Other Apps

Google has four other apps bundled in their productivity suite, which won't be covered in detail here, but for your reference, I'll explain what they are. They are not covered because this guide is meant to get you started quickly and only cover commonly used features and apps—these apps are used in some industries, but not widely adopted by most people.

Google Drawing

The name "Drawing" kind of implies that this app is for all the little artists in the world—an online app to draw to your heart's content.

While you can do drawing on the app, it's not the sort of thing you use to create the next Mona Lisa. Google is collaborative software and there's not really a big market for collaborating on art-work. Instead, Google Drawing is more suited for things like flowcharts, organizational charts, wireframes, diagrams.

Google Maps

Google Maps, unlike Google Drawing, is exactly what the name implies: a Google Map.

You can use it to add pins and layers.

Google Sites

Wouldn't you love to create a website with no coding whatsoever? Well, get out from under your rock—there are lots and lots of websites for that: Squarespace, Wix, Weebly, just to name a few.

But for those who require free and ugly, there's Google Sites!

Google Sites isn't for people who want a webpage for their business. It's for people who want a very simple page that they can collaborate with others on. It would be great, for example, if you are making a fan site for your favorite TV show, and you want everyone to be a part of it.

Google Jamboard

And finally: Jamboard.

Jamboard is basically a digital white board. If you are mounting a giant 4K TV and want to use Google, this is your solution. You can collaborate in real-time; it's perfect for business meetings and drawing cluster maps, but the hardware is too expensive for most consumers.

ABOUT THE AUTHOR

Scott La Counte is a librarian and writer. His first book, *Queit, Please: Dispatches from a Public Librarian* (Da Capo 2008) was the editor's choice for the Chicago Tribune and a Discovery title for the Los Angeles Times; in 2011, he published the YA book The N00b Warriors, which became a #1 Amazon bestseller; his most recent book is *#OrganicJesus: Finding Your Way to an Unprocessed, GMO-Free Christianity* (Kregel 2016).

He has written dozens of best-selling how-to guides on tech products.

You can connect with him at ScottDouglas.org.